KOREAN SLANGUAGE

A *FUN* VISUAL GUIDE TO KOREAN TERMS AND PHRASES BY MIKE ELLIS

GIBBS SMITH
TO ENRICH AND INSPIRE HUMANKIND

DEDICATED TO SUZANNE, VIRGINIA, MIKEY, AND PHIDGETTE

First Edition
21 20 19   5 4 3

Text © 2017 Mike Ellis
Illustrations © 2017 Rupert Bottenberg, except illustrations
of owl on pages 6, 11, 13, 41, 45, 50, 76 © 2017 locote/
Shutterstock.com; pan on pages 7, 53, 60 © 2017 Artslord/
Shutterstock.com; pie on pages 7, 48 © 2017 Brian Goff/
Shutterstock.com; hat on pages 14, 17, 21, 81 © 2017
Wiktoria Pawlak/Shutterstock.com; hand on pages 23,
25, 31 © 2017 Peter Hermes Furian/Shutterstock.com;
towel on pages 29, 60, 70 © 2017 chotwit piyapramote/
Shutterstock.com; knot on pages 37, 79 © 2017 Wiktoria
Pawlak/Shutterstock.com; wine bottle on page 54 ©
2017 grmarc/Shutterstock.com; chain on pages 78, 80
© 2017 The Polovinkin/Shutterstock.com; chimney on
page 81 © 2017 Ajay Shrivastava/Shutterstock.com

Published by
Gibbs Smith
P.O. Box 667
Layton, Utah 84041

1.800.835.4993 orders
www.gibbs-smith.com

Designed by michelvrana.com

Gibbs Smith books are printed on paper produced
from sustainable PEFC-certified forest/controlled
wood source. Learn more at www.pefc.org.
Printed and bound in Hong Kong

Library of Congress Cataloging-in-Publication Data

Names: Ellis, Mike, 1961- author.
Title: Korean slanguage : a fun visual guide
to Korean terms and phrases /
    Mike Ellis.
Description: First edition. | Layton, Utah : Gibbs Smith, [2017]
Identifiers: LCCN 2017004945 | ISBN 9781423639374 (pbk.)
Subjects: LCSH: Korean language--
Conversation and phrase books--English.
Classification: LCC PL913 .E67 2017 | DDC 495.783/421--dc23
LC record available at https://lccn.loc.gov/2017004945

CONTENTS

How to Use This Book   4
Greetings and Responses   5
Family and Friends   9
Verbs   15
Adjectives and Adverbs   22
Pronouns, Prepositions, and
    Conjunctions   35
Health and Medicine   40

Travel and Transportation   49
Food and Restaurants   58
Money and Shopping   64
Business and Labor   67
Sports and Entertainment   72
Education   77
Plants, Animals, and Nature   83
Household   92

HOW TO USE THIS BOOK

If you have always wanted to learn the basics of Korean, but traditional methods seemed overwhelming or intimidating, this is the book for you! Just follow the directions below and soon you'll be able to say dozens of words and phrases in Korean.

• Follow the illustrated prompts and practice saying the phrase quickly and smoothly.

• Emphasize the words or syllables highlighted in red.

• A strikethrough means you don't pronounce that letter or letters.

• Learn to string together words or phrases to create many more phrases.

• Draw your own pictures to help with memorization and pronunciation.

Note: This book may produce Americanized Korean.

For free sound bytes, visit slanguage.com.

Hello
안녕하세요
Annyeonghaseyo

An Young Eye Say Owl

Hi
안녕
Annyeong

An Young

Are you okay?
괜찮아요?
Gwaenchanayo?

Quinn Send Eye Oh?

I'm fine
잘 지내요
Jal jinaeyo

Tie Chew Neigh Oh

Okay
좋아요
Joayo

2 Eye Oh

On the contrary
반대로
Bandaero

Pan Day'd Oh

Please
제발
Jebal

Jay Pie

Thank you
고맙습니다
Gomabseubnida

Comb Mop Sunny Dad

Cheers!
건배!
Geonbae!

With pleasure
기쁘게
Gippeuge

You're welcome
별말씀을요
Byeolmalsseumeuryo

Cone Bay!

Key Boo Kay

Pear Mail Sue Moo

Dee Oh

Baby
아기
Agi

Ah Key

Boy
소년
Sonyeon

Soon Young

Boyfriend
남자친구
Namjachingu

Nam Debt Sing Go

Child
아이
Ai

Eye

Cousin 사촌 *Sachon*	**Set Soon**
Friend 친구 *Chingu*	**Chin Go**
Girl 소녀 *Sonyeo*	**Soon Y'Owl**
Girlfriend 여자친구 *Yeojachingu*	**Yo Debt Sing Go**

Grandchildren
손주
Sonju

Sun Due

Grandmother
할머니
Halmeoni

Hay Moe Knee

Husband
남편
Nampyeon

Nam Pea On

Marriage
결혼
Gyeolhon

G'Yo Loon

Mother 어머니 *Eomeoni*	**Oh Moe Knee**
Partner 동료 *Dongryo*	**Tongue Y'Owl**
Person 사람 *Saram*	**Saw Dam**
Sister 자매 *Jamae*	**Tom May**

To marry someone
결혼하다
Gyeolhonhada

Go Loon Hat Dad

Uncle
삼촌
Samchon

Sam Soon

Wedding anniversary
결혼 기념일
Gyeolhon ginyeomil

Go Loon Kin Yum Eel

Woman
여자
Yeoja

Yo Tap

To be afraid
두렵다
Duryeopda

2D Up Dad

To be born
태어나다
Taeeonada

Tay Own Uh Dad

To believe
믿다
Mitda

Meet Dad

To bend
굽히다
Gupida

Goo Pea Dad

16 VERBS

To bring
가져오다
Gajyeooda

To choke
숨이 막히다
Sumi makhida

To create
창조하다
Changjohada

To deceive
속이다
Sokida

Guy Joe Uh Dad

Sue Me Mack Key Dad

Tongue 2 Hat Dad

Sew Key Dad

To dress
옷을 입다
Oseul ipda

To feel
느끼다
Neukkida

To forget
잇다
Itda

To hide
숨기다
Sumgida

Ooh Silly Dad

New Key Dad

Eat Dad

Assume Key Dad

18 VERBS

To inhale
들이 마시다
Deuri masida

2D Ma She Dad

To know
알다
Alda

Eye Dad

To leave
떠나다
Tteonada

Donut Dad

To remember
기억하다
Gieokhada

Key Yolk Uh Dad

To repair
고치다
Gochida

To see
보다
Boda

To send
보내다
Bonaeda

To spread
쫙 펴다
Jjwak pyeoda

Coat See Dad

Bow Dad

Bow Neigh Dad

Chuck Pea Oh Dad

20 VERBS

To unfold
펴다
Pyeoda

To use
사용하다
Sayonghada

To wait
기다리다
Gidarida

Pea Oh Dad

Sigh Oh Hat Dad

Key Dolly Dad

ADJECTIVES AND ADVERBS

Arrogant
거만한
Geomanhan

Go Man Hand

At first
처음에
Cheoeume

Toe May

Before
이전에
Ijeone

Eat Sew Neigh

Beside
옆에
Yeope

Yo Pay

Better 더 좋은 *Deo joeun*	**How Tune** ♪
Certainly 확실히 *Hwaksilhi*	**Hack See Dee**
Crazy 미친 *Michin*	**Meat Sin**
Dead 죽은 *Jugeun*	**2 Goon**

Empty
텅 빈
Teong bin

Tongue Bin

Engaged
약혼한
Yakhonhan

Yacht Coo Nan

Enormous
거대한
Geodaehan

Go Day Hand

Far
먼
Meon

Mund

Fortunately
다행히도
Dahaenghido

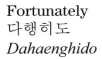 

Highness Knee Doe

Happy
행복한
Haengbokhan

Hen Boo Con

Heavy
무거운
Mugeoun

Moo Cone

Here
여기
Yeogi

Yolk Key

High
높은
Nopeun

No Pen

Auto Kay

How
어떻게
Eotteohke

Idiotic
백치의
Paegchiui

Pick T.A.

Tin She Me Ah Knee

Insincere
진심이 아닌
Jinsimi anin

Long 긴 *Gin*	**Keen**
Many 많이 *Mani*	**My Knee**
Mature 성숙한 *Seongsukhan*	**Song Sue Con**
Mood 기분 *Gibun*	**Key Boon**

More
더 많은
Deo maneun

Doe Man Den

New
새로운
Saeroun

Say Loon

Next
다음의
Daeumui

Towel May

Old
늙은
Neulgeun

Knee Gun

Ordinary
평범한
Pyeongbeomhan

 P'Young Bomb Man

Quite
상당히
Sangdanghi

Sung Dung He

Sad
슬픈
Seulpeun

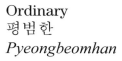 See Poon

Same
같은
Gateun

Cotton

Silent
조용한
Joyonghan

Silently
조용히
Joyonghi

Single
하나의
Hanaui

Slowly
천천히
Cheoncheonhi

Toy Young Hen

Toy You Knee

Hand Nye

Tongue Tongue Knee

Stupid
바보 같은
Babo gateun

Pa Boo Got Ten

Then
그때의
Geuttaeui

Good Day

There
거기
Geogi

Call Key

Thick
두꺼운
Dukkeoun

2 Cone

Tired
피곤한
Pigonhan

Pea Go Nun

Together
함께
Hamkke

Hum Kay

Weak
약한
Yakhan

Yacht Con

Well-dressed
옷을 잘입은
Oseul jal ibeun

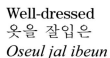

Ooh See Tally Boon

Where 어디 *Eodi*	**Awe Deep**
Whole 전체의 *Jeoncheui*	**Tongue Tear**
Why 왜 *Wae*	**Way**
Young 젊은 *Jeolmeun*	**Tie You Men**

PRONOUNS, PREPOSITIONS, AND CONJUNCTIONS

After 후에 *Hue*	**Who Way**
Against 맞서 *Matseo*	**Mats How**
All 모든 *Modeun*	**Moe Den**
Also 또한 *Ttohan*	**2 On**

Because
때문에
Ttaemune

 Tay Moo Neigh

But
하지만
Hajiman

 Hot Say Man

I
나
Na

 Knot

In
안에
Ane

 Ah Neigh

In front of
앞에
Ape

Up Pay

Outside
밖에
Bakke

Pa Kay

We
우리
Uri

Julie

Where
어디로
Eodiro

Oh Dee Doe

Who
누구
Nugu

New Goo

Why
왜
Wae

Way

You
너
Neo

No

Ankle 발목 *Balmok*	**Pile Moe**
Arm 팔 *Pal*	**Pile**
Bath 목욕 *Mokyok*	 **Moe Key Oh**
Beard 수염 *Suyeom*	**See Y'Owl**

Blood
피
Pi

Pea

Cigarette
담배
Dambae

Dam Bay

Cold
감기
Gamgi

Come Key

Disease
병
Pyeong

P'Young

Eye
눈
Nun

Fingernail
손톱
Sontop

Fist
주먹
Jumeok

Flu
독감
Doggam

Noon

Sun Toe

2 Ma

2 Cam

Foot
발
Bal

Pile

Sewn

Hand
손
Son

Head
머리
Meori

More Reed

Heart
심장
Simjang

Shim Tongue

Incubation		Champ Boo Key
잠복기		
Jambokgi		
Infection		Come Y'Owl
감염		
Gamyeom		
Injection		2 Sat
주사		
Jusa		
Medicine		Yeah
약		
Yak		

Neck
목
Mok

Moo'k

Nose
코
Ko

Comb

Pain
고통
Gotong

Go Tone

Pharmacy
약국
Yakguk

Yacht Go

Razor
면도칼
Myeondokal

Me End Doe Kite

Sick
병자의
Pyeongjaui

P'Young Die Eh

Skin
피부
Pibu

Pea Boo

Soap
비누
Binu

Pea New

Specimen
표본
Pyobon

 P'Yo Bone

Stomach
위
Wi

We

Towel
수건
Sugeon

Sue Gone

  Pie Eat Doe Say

Virus
바이러스
Baireoseu

TRAVEL AND TRANSPORTATION

Airplane
비행기
Bihaenggi

Pea Yankee

Bakery
제과점
Jegwajeom

Take What Dumb

Bookstore
서점
Seojeom

Sew Sum

Border
국경
Gukgyeong

Kook Y'Owl

Cafeteria
구내 식당
Gunae sikdang

 Cone Nay Sick Dad

Castle
성
Seong

♪Song

City
도시
Dosi

 **Toe See**

Flight
비행
Bihaeng

Pea Hang

Gasoline
휘발유
Hwiballyu

He Buy You

Germany
독일
Dokil

 Toe Keel

To land
착륙하다
Chakryukhada

Tongue You Cut Dad

Mailbox
우체통
Uchetong

You Tic Tong

Movie theater
영화관
Yeonghwagwan

Young How G'Wan

Nationality
국적
Gukjeok

Cook Tough

One-way ticket
편도 티켓
Pyeondo tiket

Pan Doe Tee Kate

Port
항구
Hanggu

Hang Go

Province 지방 *Jibang*	**Chee Bang**
Restaurant 식당 *Sikdang*	**Sick Dang**
Road 도로 *Doro*	 **Toad Oh**
Russian 러시아인 *Reosiain*	 **Row She Wine**

Ship 배 *Bae*	**Pay** **Poe Toe**
Sidewalk 보도 *Bodo*	
State 주 *Ju*	**2**
Store 상점 *Sangjeom*	**Sung Tum**

Train
기차
Gicha

Train station
기차역
Gichayeok

Van
밴
Baen

Vehicle
차량
Charyang

Key Tap

Key Tie Yacht

Pen

Teddy Young

Wheel
바퀴
Bakwi

West
서쪽
Seojjok

Western
서양의
Seoyangui

World
세계
Segye

Pack We

Sun Toe

Soy Young Yay

Say Gay

I'd like . . .
나는 . . . 원한다
Naneun . . . wonhanda

Nah Nen . . . Woe

None Dad

Do you have . . . ?
너는 . . . 있니?
Neonun . . . inni?

No Nin . . . Inn Knee?

Beef
소고기
Sogogi

Sew Goo Key

Beer
맥주
Maekju

May 2

Bread
빵
Ppang

Pan

Butter
버터
Peoteo

Putt Towel

Cabbage
양배추
Yangbaechu

Young Bay 2

Carrot
당근
Danggeun

Tongue Goon

Dessert
후식
Husik

Who She

Fish
생선
Saengseon

Sing Song

Fork
포크
Pokeu

Poke Kay

Onion
양파
Yangpa

Young Pa

Bean
콩
Kong

Cone

Pepper
고추
Gochu

Go Choo

Radish
무
Mu

Moo

Rice 쌀 *Ssal*	**Sigh**
Salt 소금 *Sogeum*	**Soak 'Em**
Sausage 소시지 *Sosiji*	 **Sew Sheet Say**
Wine 포도주 *Podoju*	 **Poe Dudes You**

To buy
사다
Sada

Sad Dad

Check
수표
Supyo

Soup Yo

Clerk
점원
Jeomwon

Some Hun

Credit
신용
Sinyong

Sin Y'Own

Expensive
비싼
Bissan

Pea Sand

Kiosk
매점
Maejeom

Maid Sum

Money
돈
Don

Don't

Vending machine
자판기
Japangi

Japan Key

Accounting
회계
Hoegye

Hay Get

Carpenter
목수
Moksu

Mocha Sue

Desk
책상
Chaeksang

Jake Sun

Factory
공장
Gongjang

Coon Jan

Farmer
농부
Nongbu

General
장군
Janggun

Housewife
주부
Jubu

Mailman
우체부
Uchebu

Noon Boo

Tongue Goon

Chew Boo

You Tee Boo

Newspaper
신문
Sinmun

Seen Moon

Note
메모
Memo

May Moe

Politician
정치인
Jeongchiin

Tongue Teen

Printer
프린터
Peurinteo

Put Inn Towel

Thief
도둑
Doduk

Doe 2

Tourist
여행객
Yeohaenggaek

Yo Hen Gay

Vacation
휴가
Hyuga

Hue Got

SPORTS AND ENTERTAINMENT

Ball
공
Gong

Gong

Bell
벨
Bel

Pale

Choir
성가대
Seonggadae

Sun God Day

Detective story
탐정 소설
Tamjeong soseol

Tom Tongue Sue's Are

Dinner party
저녁 파티
Jeonyeok pati

Tone Young Pat Tee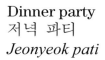

Fishing
낚시
Naksi

Nock Say

Football
미식축구
Misigchuggu

Me Seek 2 Go

Kite
연
Yeon

Young

Poem
시
Si

 See

Rugby
럭비
Leokbi

Lug Pea

Soccer
축구
Chukgu

Chew Go

Statue
동상
Dongsang

Tongue Sang

Surfing
써핑
Seoping

S'Up Ping

Swimming
수영
Suyeong

See Y'Owl

Walking
걷기
Geotgi

Coat Key

Angle
각도
Gakdo

Book
책
Chaek

Calculator
계산기
Gyesangi

Degree
학위
Hagwi

Cat Doe

Chain

Kay Sun Key

Hack Key

To divide
나누다
Nanuda

To erase
지우다
Jiuda

Geometry
기하학
Gihahak

Grammar
문법
Munbeop

Knot New Dad

T'You Dad

Key Ha Ha

Moon Bob

History 역사 *Yeoksa*	**Yolk Sat**
Homework 숙제 *Sugje*	**Suit Say**
Math 수학 *Suhak*	**Sue Hag**
Notebook 공책 *Gongchaek*	**Cone Chain**

Physics
물리학
Mullihak

Problem
문제
Munje

Psychology
심리학
Simnihak

Semester
학기
Hakgi

Moo Lee Yeah

Moon Say

Chimney Ha

Hat Key

Student
학생
Haksaeng

Hack Sing

Subtraction
빼기
Ppaegi

Pay Key

Sum
합계
Hapgye

Happy Kay

Symbol
상징
Sangjing

Sand Sing

PLANTS, ANIMALS, AND NATURE

Air
공기
Gonggi

Cone Key

Bee
벌
Beol

Ball

Dandelion
민들레
Mindeulle

Mean Do Lay

Dog
개
Gae

Kay

Fire
불
Bul

Fog
안개
Angae

Giraffe
기린
Girin

Ice
얼음
Eoreum

Pool

Bun Kay

Key Rinse

Are Yum

Insect
곤충
Gonchung

Cone Tune

Island
섬
Seom

Sum

It's cool
시원하다
Siwonhada

Show Not Dad

It's hot
덥다
Deopda

Doe Dad

Lake
호수
Hosu

Hoe Sue

Light
빛
Bit

Beet

Mountain
산
San

Sun

Mouse
쥐
Jwi

Tweet

Rain
비
Bi

Pea

To rain
비가 오다
Biga oda

Pea Cot Oh Dad

River
강
Gang

Kong

Rose
장미
Jangmi

Tongue Me

Smoke
연기
Yeongi

Young **Key**

Snow
눈
Nun

Noon

To snow
눈이 오다
Nuni oda

Noon Yee Oh Dad

Space
우주
Uju

Ooh Chew

Spider
거미
Geomi

Go Me

Surface
표면
Pyomyeon

P'Yuma Young

Swan
백조
Baekjo

Pay Joe

Tortoise
거북이
Geobugi

Go Boo Key

Tree
나무
Namu

Nam Mo

Tulip
튤립
Tyullip

2 Leap

Weather
날씨
Nalssi

Nile See

Candle
양초
Yangcho

Yang Toe

Corridor
복도
Bokdo

Poke Doe

Dish
접시
Jeobsi

Top See

Door
문
Mun

Moon

Furniture
가구
Gagu

Guy Go

Laundry
빨래
Ppallae

Pa Lay

Light bulb
전구
Jeongu

Tongue Go

Matches
성냥
Seongnyang

Song Yang

Mirror
거울
Geoul

Coal

Pillow
베개
Begae

Pay Gay

Remote control
리모컨
Rimokeon

Ream Moo Con

Stairs
계단
Gyedan

Kay Dan

Stove
난로
Nallo

Nan Low

Towel
수건
Sugeon

Sue Gone

Vacuum cleaner
진공청소기
Jingongcheongsogi

Sing Goon Sung Sue Key

Washing machine
세탁기
Setakgi

Set Tag Key